Piano Development L2

Composed by Giovanni Andreani

First published in 2022 by
GA
Via Colombo 4, 24061 Albano Sant'Alessandro, BG, Italy
Copyright © Giovanni Andreani 2018

ISBN 978-88-314710-1-5
All rights reserved. No part of this publication may be reproduced, stored in any retrieval system, or transmitted, in any form or by any means, electronic, mechanical, photocopying, recording or otherwise, without the prior written permission of the copyright owner.

*In memory of Pál Kadosa,
for his enlightening contribution to piano pedagogy*

"Music is nourishment, and a comforting elixir. Music multiplies the beauty of life and all its values"

— Zoltán Kodály

PREFACE

A comprehensive and effective programme must consider all of the possible sectors in which the student's skills and competence can develop, which fall into two main categories: musicianship[1] and instrumental skills. The Music Method Project (MusMP) comprises the Piano Method Project (PMP), related to the development of instrumental skills, and the Musicianship Method Project (MMP), related to musicianship development.

While musicianship will develop slightly when studying an instrument, scientifically well-programmed musicianship development will be the primary factor for excellent instrumental improvement. As a consequence, some areas of development in PMP will be performed at the piano while others will have to be undertaken with or without the subsidiary use of a piano (see footnote n. 2).

The more the proposed activities are varied and systematically organised, the better the development of skills and competence will be. As a consequence, the contrast between different activities will stimulate the student's interest, which will result in greater emotional involvement, a higher level of participation, and a more dynamic attitude.

Differentiation must also consider the time terms that are intrinsic to all specific Development Areas.

In PMP, the following time terms have been conceived:

- Instant Term [IT] - from 5 seconds to 15 minutes
- Daily Term [DT] - 15 minutes to 6 hours
- Very Short Term [VST] - 1 day to 1 week
- Short Term [ST] – 2 weeks
- Medium Term [MT] – 1 month
- Long Term [LT] – 2 to 4 months
- Very Long Term [VLT] – 4 to 6 months

Within a well-differentiated programme, the student should deal simultaneously with activities that require different time terms that derive from different areas. Short-term activities should outnumber those that are expected to take longer.

---

1   Musicianship should be considered essential for the student's improvement; in many cases it is not, for many reasons, among which lies the complexity to plan a specific curriculum.

Piano Development L2

Although it is undoubtedly important for the student to simultaneously manage various activities as part of the different areas of development, any new activity should be gradually introduced.

Within PMP, Piano Development (PD) is the only area that should be constantly active: all other areas can be started according to the teacher's discretion, in relation to the student's aptitude, specific needs, expectations, and so forth.

In PMP, the Development Areas are (with their corresponding time terms):

- Piano Development [VST]
- Sing & Play[2] [VST]
- Note Reading[2] [IT] - [VST]
- Listen & Play[2] [IT] - [VST]
- Sight Reading [IT]
- Technique Exercises [ST] - [VLT]
- Scales & Arpeggios [ST] - [VLT]
- Études [MT] - [VLT]
- Quick Studies [IT]
- Piano Improvisation [IT] - [VST]
- Piano Composition [VST] - [MT]
- Solo Repertoire [MT] - [VLT]
- Piano Duet Repertoire [MT] - [VLT]
- Chamber Music Repertoire [MT] - [VLT]

Some activities will be achieved after a very short time whereas others will require longer. Moreover, after some activities have been attained, a maintenance programme will be necessary: this is true for some technical exercises, scales, and arpeggios, and some selected études and repertoire pieces, etc.

---

2   Transitional areas of correlation between Musicianship and Instrumental Development.

INTRODUCTION

Piano Development (PD) is, throughout the PMP Development Areas, the main framework around which all other Development Areas orbit; it has been conceived to help piano teachers achieve a profound view of their student's improvements while guiding them throughout the higher levels of piano playing.

PD is divided into a first set of 20 levels and the student should be working on two different and consecutive levels at the same time.

As progress is made, a new Development Area may be added: the more areas the student manages, the more profoundly competence and skills will grow[1]; nonetheless, PD should be the only Development Area on which the student will be working constantly.

PD consists of short pieces that the student will have to prepare for the following lesson; how these pieces will be mastered is an issue to be pre-emptively clarified in order to positively monitor the student's progress. Therefore, the teacher will have to determine in advance which criteria to adopt when evaluating each piece and assigning a new one in its place. Criteria for when to pass from one level to another should also be established in advance[2].

The general complexity expressed at each level of PD does not have to be comparable to the difficulty of other areas simultaneously studied, especially if related to repertoire. Indeed, the student may find him/herself studying a repertoire piece that is much more difficult than is expressed by the level required in PD: this would be perfectly appropriate while the contrary would, surely be unfitting. The time term of PD is classified as VST[3] while a repertoire piece may be classified from MT to VLT; therefore, the latter can be more complex.

Using this Book

There is no strict way in which to use this book; it can be adopted for various purposes accordingly. Nevertheless, its main purpose is to be part of the PMP. The teacher who wishes to follow the PMP principles will find a rich collection of musical material, all PMP resources were also conceived within a specific plan inherently designed into an effective and comprehensive programme.

---

1   As referred to in the preface.

2   Each teacher should plan and compile their own methodological programme, according to the students needs, without having to follow a rigid and predetermined programme, identical for all students: for this reason any new development area should be started when the teacher feels it is appropriate for each student.

3   Refer to preface for time terms.

Rhythm

The student will be required to interpret the following durations[4] and rhythmic patterns:

At this level all melodic lines are played by one hand at the time with no superimposition of a second melody or any other kind of melodic structure.

Some piecese will be played exclusevely with one hand while others will require the use of both hands: in this case the melody will pass from one hand to the other; a dotted line connecting the melody through the two staves will help visualizing the correct melodic outline[5]. When playing a melody without a contrapunctual line the student's inner hearing and sense of rhythm and control of durations[4] will consistently develope; consequentely a sense of metre will strongly improve.

By following the PMP principles the student will be working on PD L1 or PD L3 together with this level; in the latter case, the student will be dealing with a mixed set of pieces composed for two hands playing simultaneously as well as pieces for two hands performing one only melody.

Notes and Hand-Positions

The student should be able to find and play any key in any octave by matching the key's name (or names) with its position on the keyboard.

The student should be able to name the notes from the staff with both the G clef and the F clef; reading fluently is not required for starting this level, as it is the ability to determine the first note of each piece that is needed (the 'Note Reading' series may be carried out contextually to improve pure note-reading skills).

---

4   Refer to 'List of Abbreviations' at the end of the introduction.

5   A melodic line passing from one hand to the other can be found in many cases in the keyboard literature; as an example, the inner voice (or voices) from a fugue, generally with more than two parts, may be performed alternately by the two hands.

Fingering

The student should be able to understand and adopt fingering indications; although at this level, all pieces are composed using mainly three notes per hand, various intervals between the notes and different combinations of fingers will occur.

Time Signatures

At this level, the following time signatures will be found:

$$\frac{2}{4} \quad \frac{3}{4} \quad \frac{4}{4} \quad \frac{6}{8}$$

Some Teaching Directions

All starting notes should be identified and labelled; when doing so, the octave number should always be included: There are several methods that combine note names and pitch octave numbers; in 'Scientific Pitch Notation' (SPN), for example, so-called 'middle C' is combined with the number 4 to identify its pitch octave, thus defining the note as C_4[6]. When assigning a new piece, the student should attempt to identify and label the starting note with the teacher's assistance.

Methodological Approach to these Pieces

It must be remembered that preparation for playing a piece must involve the issues that the student will have to deal with when practising alone without the teacher's support; at this level, solving preparation problems requires answering the following four questions, as it can be seen in Fig. 1:

    I.   Which hand begins to play the melody?
    II. Which is the starting note for each hand?
    III. Which finger plays each starting note?
    IV. Which other notes/fingers are required to be played?

All four of these points should never be taken for granted and, when solved, preparation will be

---

6   In some countries C_4 is named C_3 or other pitch notation systems may be adopted.

complete and the hand-positions obtained: the student will now be ready to perform the piece and concentrate on another set of details while playing.

Fig. 1

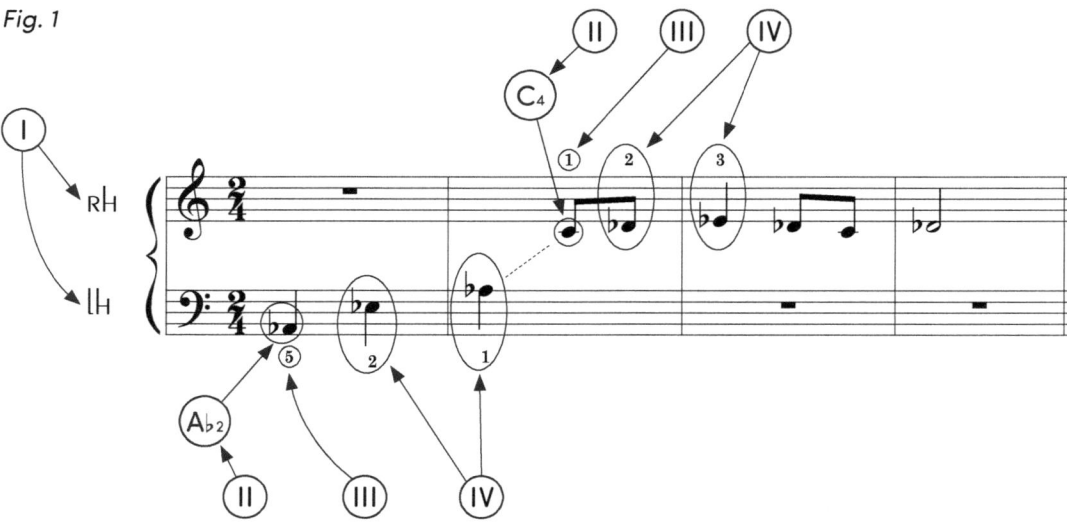

To facilitate adaptation to the required hand positions, before attempting to play the piece, the student may improvise some short motifs, as shown in fig. 2 (considering, for example, the piece as in fig. 1):

Fig. 2

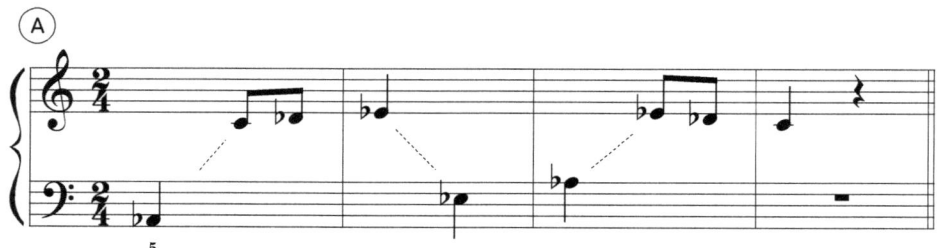

Accidentals

At the very first stage, it is not necessary to introduce the full meaning of symbols such as the sharp, the flat, and the natural; as the student begins to learn to link, for example, the note name G with a specific key on the keyboard, the same can be done for keys named G♯ and A♭, etc. This linking may also include C♭-B, B♯-C, F♭-E and E♯-F note/key combinations.

The specific meaning of these symbols may eventually be introduced later on, according to the theory programme adopted.

Hand Positions

A fundamental pedagogical principle proposed here is to avoid imposing a C-centred hand position as standard, while also steering clear of favouring one single clef over the other; the use of just a few hand-positions is also avoided. The student will be exploring the whole keyboard while gradually experiencing a variety of different hand-positions.

This approach should not discourage those teachers who are used to only one or a few positions for a long term: having reached the minimum prerequisites recommended for adopting this textbook, the only main issue when assigning a new piece will be to identify, for each hand, the starting note and the finger associated with it; by finding the remaining notes and their finger combinations, the required hand positions will be assumed. One important advantage is that the hands will be able to assume different kinds of positions, from those with fingers covering only the white keys, to those with the hand pushed in a forward position and the fingers inserted between the black keys, up to those with the hand in a stretched position or in a squeezed, compressed position, among others. By constantly finding various new hand positions, the student will develop remarkable mental agility and improved equilibrium within his/her physical relationship with the keyboard.

Metronome

Metronome marks mainly suggest the pace at which a piece should be played. Playing in time to a metronome, however, is much more difficult than it may seem; it may be more productive to play duets in order to practise a fluent and uniform pace.

When playing with a metronome, the student is required to constantly adjust his/her own pace to match the metronome's pulse whereas, when playing with another person, the adjustment is mutual.

Improvising Chamber Music

We encourage all teachers to improvise duets with their students as an alternative way of playing these and other pieces. Improvised duets may not only be performed as a three or four hand piano ensemble: once the student is able to play a piece from this series, improvising duets with alternative kinds of instruments, including percussion and the use of the voice, among others, should always be encouraged. Changing roles is also important: the teacher or another student can play the piece while the student improvises an accompaniment or another musical structure; it is important, in some cases, to use an instrument easy to play, such a percussion instrument, for example.

Key Signatures

At this level, all pieces are presented without a key signature; most of them, however, are not related to C major or its relative minor key: accidentals, therefore, will appear for the moment, 'in itinere', for three reasons: the first is to accustom the student to key alterations, making them clear every time they are needed; the second reason is that these pieces, despite the fact they are mostly tonally identifiable, are nevertheless composed of only a small number of notes: it would then be possible to play a piece in D minor, for example, without ever having to play a B flat; and, thirdly, the student, in having to experience many possible hand positions, should be offered the opportunity to play, for example, in the key of E♭ minor, or any other key without having to know all the rules underlying the tonal structures.

Directions for the Teacher

Each assigned piece should be prepared and fully mastered for the next lesson (usually the following week).

When assigning a new piece, the student and teacher together should pinpoint the first notes played by each hand and write them down with their pitch octave number. No other note names should be written down.

Finger numbers are provided for the hand to be situated in a particular position: no other finger numbers should be added. If the teacher decides to require different fingering this should be clearly established before assigning the work.

The student, when following these procedures alone, while practising, should be able to solve all problems related to the preparation of the piece, and know how to interpret all involved rhythmic patterns, durations, and time signatures included therein; consequently, the student should be able, by practising during the period until the following lesson, to perform the piece with a high degree of competency.

Moving to a New Piece

When evaluating whether a piece is to be considered as having been mastered and therefore archived and replaced by another one, a set of criteria should be considered as evaluating parameters; according to each student's poise, level of musicianship, general aptitude, and so forth, more or fewer criteria may be considered.

The main mandatory criterion could be:

- The piece must be played with flow and no interruption
- Rhythms and durations must be accurate
- Notes must be correct
- Fingers must be respected
- Playing should be realised in a relaxed and anxiety-free way

Further criteria that may apply according to the teacher's discretion, could be, among others:

- Hairpin diminuendos should be respected
- Dynamics and crescendo hairpins should be respected
- Articulation and accent signs should be respected
- The tempo may not be accurate as indicated, although the mood and the tempo itself should be appropriate to the style of the piece
- Phrasing and a sense of metre should be expressed

Once established, the criterion chosen for evaluating all performances must be strictly maintained throughout the level; if the student's performance does not meet the predetermined criterion, the piece should remain as an objective for the next lesson; when the performance meets the established criterion for a positive evaluation, the piece will be archived and replaced by one within the same level.

Moving to a New Level

Although it is always the teacher who plans and is responsible for the proposed programme, if the PMP principles are being followed, PD should be adopted by using two consecutive levels simultaneously.

When selecting a level for the first time, the teacher will identify the most appropriate stage for the student. The student will then begin from the level previous to that selected and, after the first few pieces have been studied, the first chosen level may be added: the student will therefore be simultaneously working on two consecutive levels.

The number of pieces assigned from each level should comprise more from the lower of the two levels while maintaining the following proportions:

\	Piano Development Weekly Assigned Work (no. of pieces)			
Task Type	*Pieces from Lower Level*	*Pieces from Higher Level*	*Total Pieces Assigned*	*Pieces Evaluated Weekly*
Light	1	1	2	1
Medium	2	1	3	1 or 2
Intense	3	1 or 2	4 or 5	2 or 3
Demanding	4	2	6	2 to 4

It is important to not evaluate all assigned pieces at each lesson: as a consequence, the non-played pieces will settle within the time before the next lesson; this is an important issue due to the fact that not all of the pieces may be well prepared for every following lesson, for different reasons, that are not always dependent on the student's diligence.

Three pieces are a sizeable task to deal with within a week, considering that each lesson will include activities from other areas as well; we therefore recommend assigning this number of pieces, as a medium task, as can be seen in the above table.

Before evaluating whether a student can move to the next level, at least the first 20 pieces should be practised.

If the student is consistently dealing with between one and three pieces (medium task), then a basic set consisting of at least the first 25 pieces should be practised before evaluating whether the student can move to the next level.

If the student is consistently dealing with more than three pieces (intense or demanding task), then a basic set consisting of at least the first 30 pieces should be practised before evaluating whether the student can move to the next level.

After having completed the defined set of pieces required before evaluating whether the student can move to the next level, the teacher should then use a predetermined criteria to evaluate whether such a condition exists; two procedures, among other possible solutions, are described here (for the case of a student dealing with a medium task):

Example 1: from piece 25, the teacher analyses the last five archived pieces and, when the average percentage of the positively performed pieces on the first required occasion is at least equal to 80%, the student will move to the next level.

Example 2: from piece 25, the teacher analyses the last four archived pieces and, when the last four pieces in a row are evaluated as positively performed on the first required occasion, the student will move to the next level.

As stated before, the majority of pieces assigned should be from the lower of the two levels, from which the student will move to a piece that is two levels ahead.

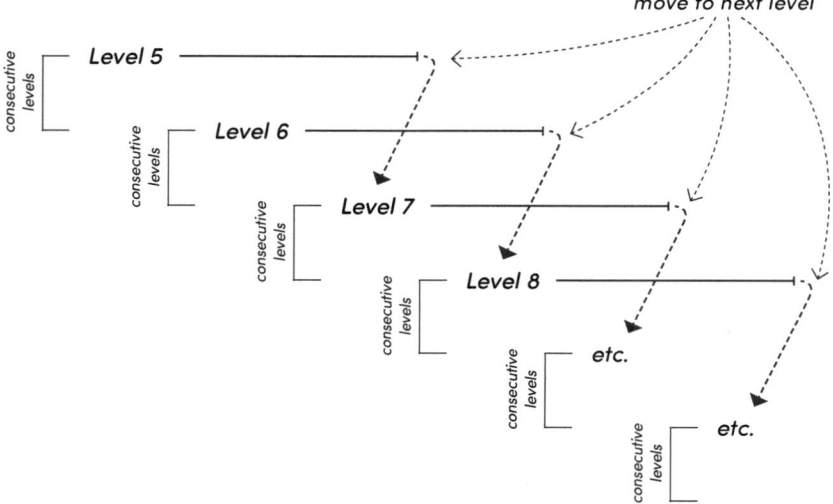

Monitoring

The teacher should keep a detailed record of all activities carried out at each lesson; this will provide an important amount of data that will make the teacher aware of the student's progress and improvements.

Although the teacher may select and assign a new piece according to a personal order, it is important to do so in the correct numerical order. All pieces are set into groups, each of which contains a specific detail or a particular problem that will recur cyclically.

Although the pieces will never all be at exactly the same level of difficulty, they are conceived to meet characteristics that will distinguish them as part of the specific level defined by this book.

LIST OF ABBREVIATIONS

MusMP: Music Method Project, which includes MMP and IMP

MMP: Musicianship Method Project

IMP: Instrumental Method Project

PMP: Piano Method Project, a part of IMP

PD: Piano Development, a Development Area of PMP

Development Area: a branch, a sector in which specific skills are developed

Activity: a piece, an exercise, anything from a one-bar rhythm to a whole movement of a sonata or anything else, provided that it is a whole defined item. An activity is part of a specific Development Area

Objective: a specific task intended to be accomplished according to a predetermined period of time. An objective is a part of or can coincide with an entire activity[7]

Duration[8]: any rhythmic value equal to or greater than the pulse value

Rhythmic pattern: a sequence of rhythmic values usually smaller than the pulse value and perceived as a structure generally fitting one[9] pulse

---

[7] As an example, a thirty-two bar piece is divided in two sections of sixteen bars each: only one section is required to be studied for the time arranged with the student. In this case the whole piece is the activity while the single section is the objective. Let's say that in addition to the piece's section, one scale, one arpeggio and one study are also assigned: all of these are different objectives from activities from different development areas.

[8] Duration also refers to the lenght of time of a piece.

[9] Rhythmic patterns may also fit multiple beat durations; the most common ones, however, fit one or two beats.

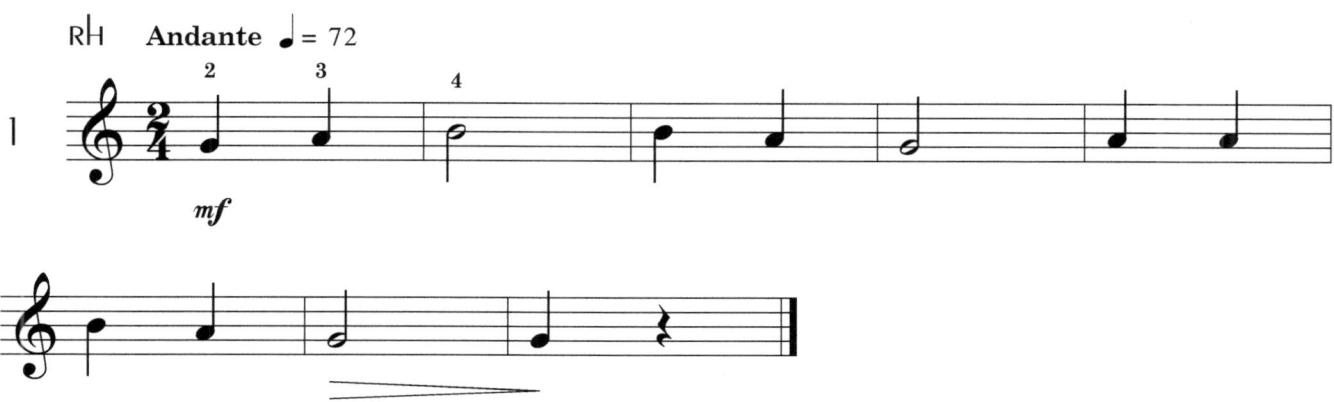
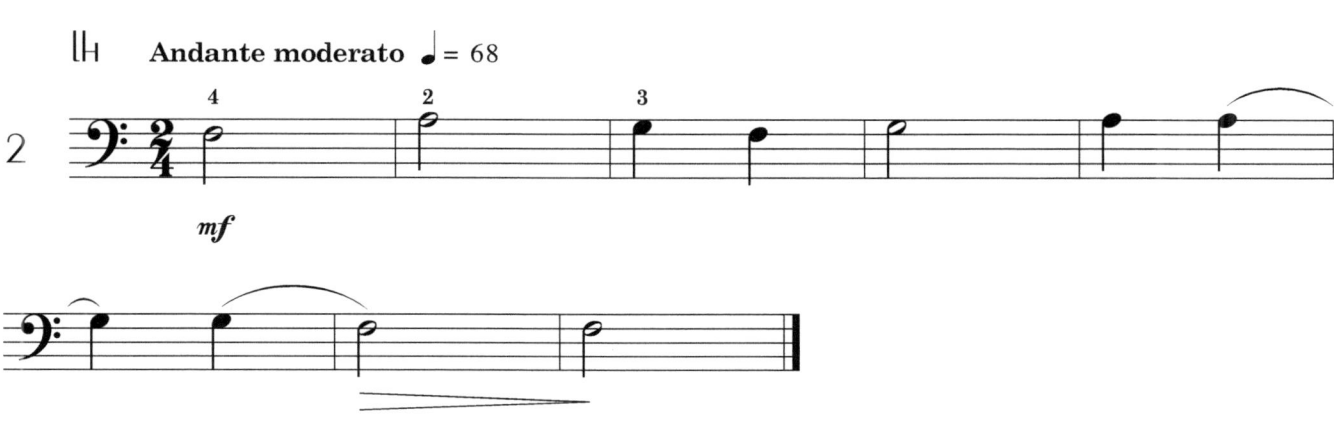

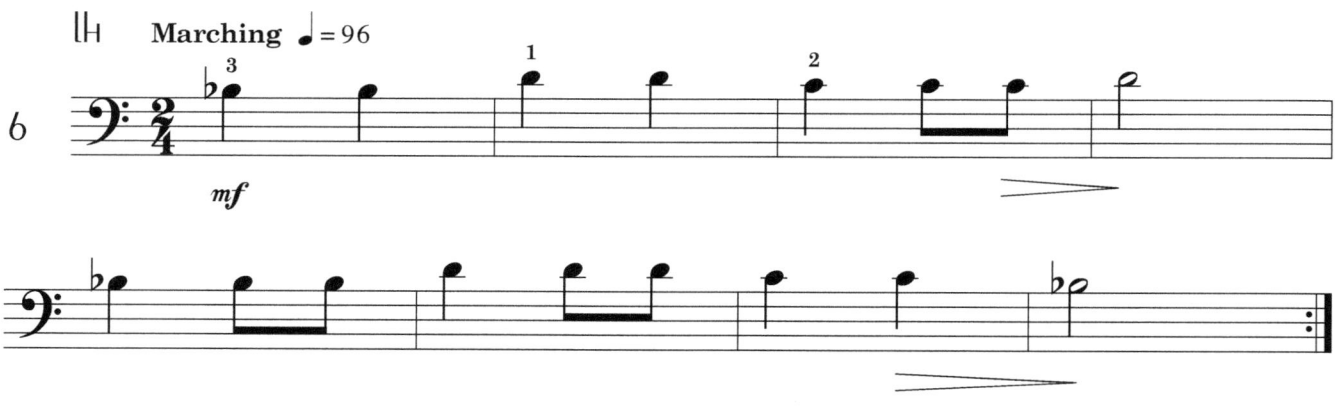

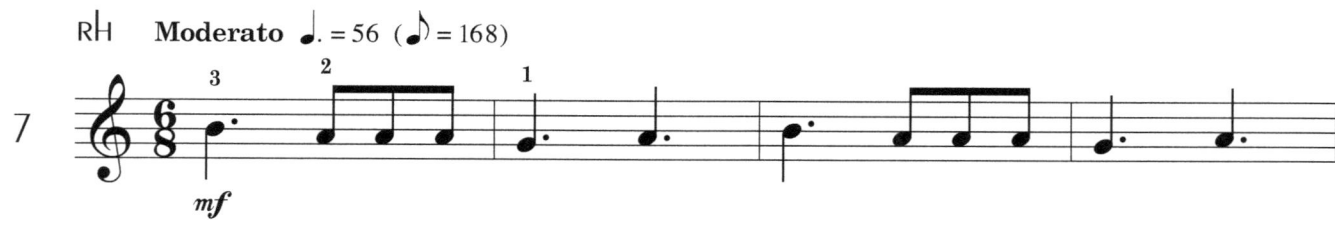

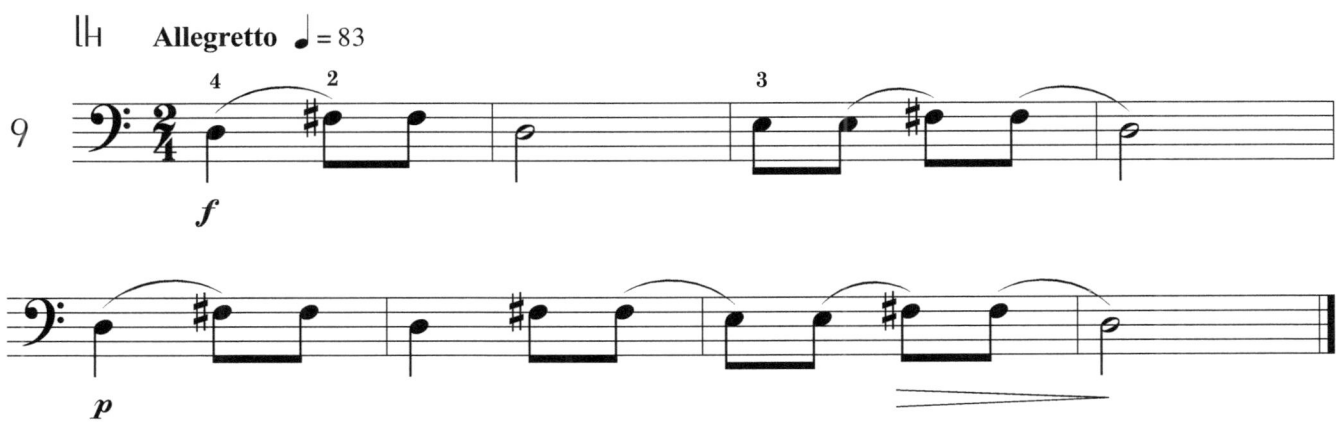

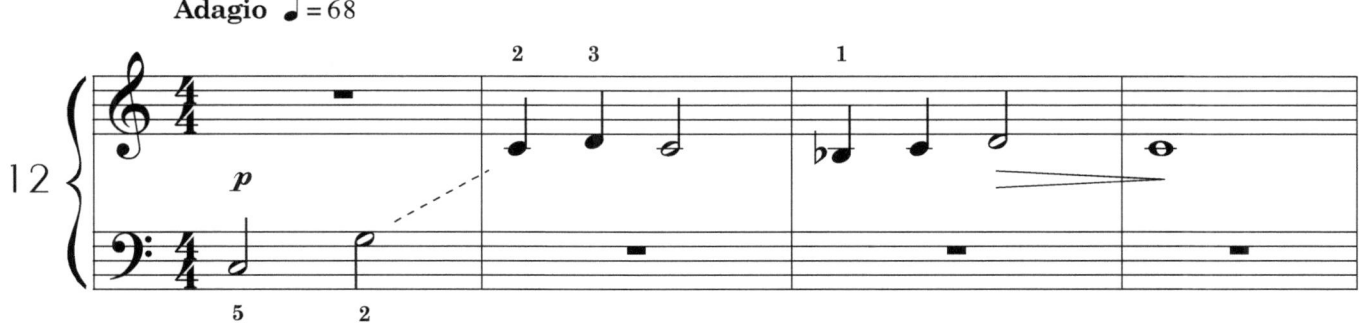

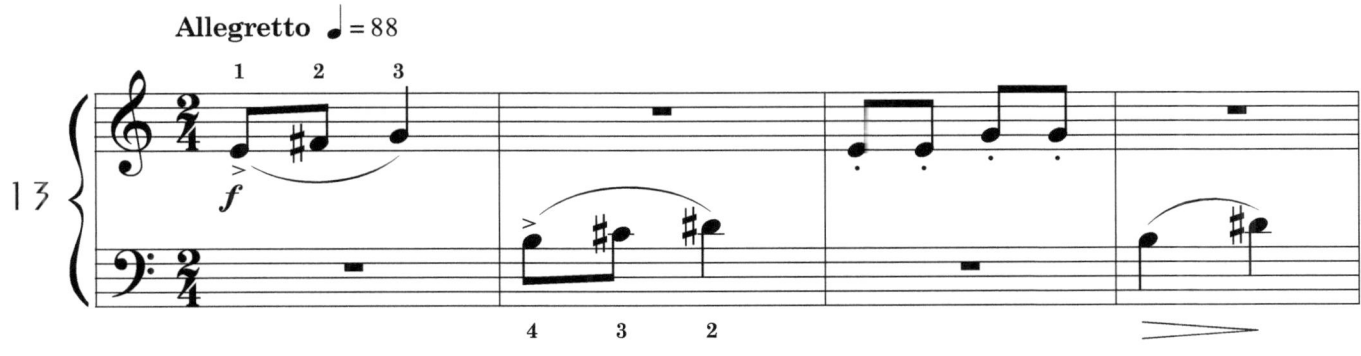
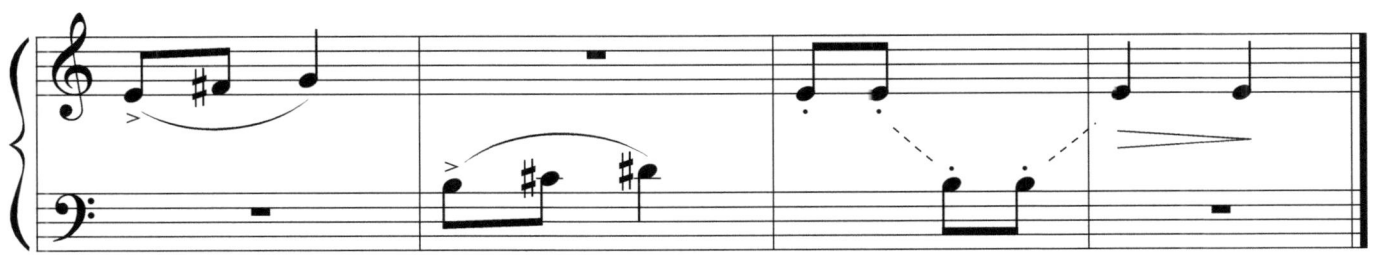

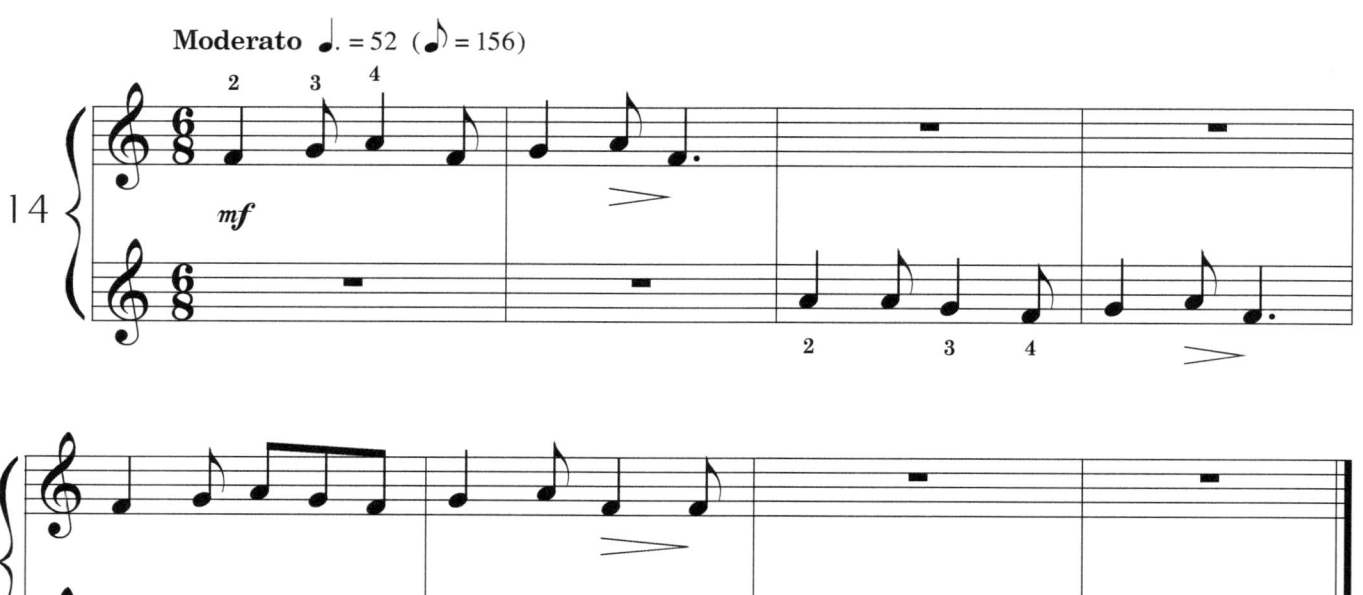

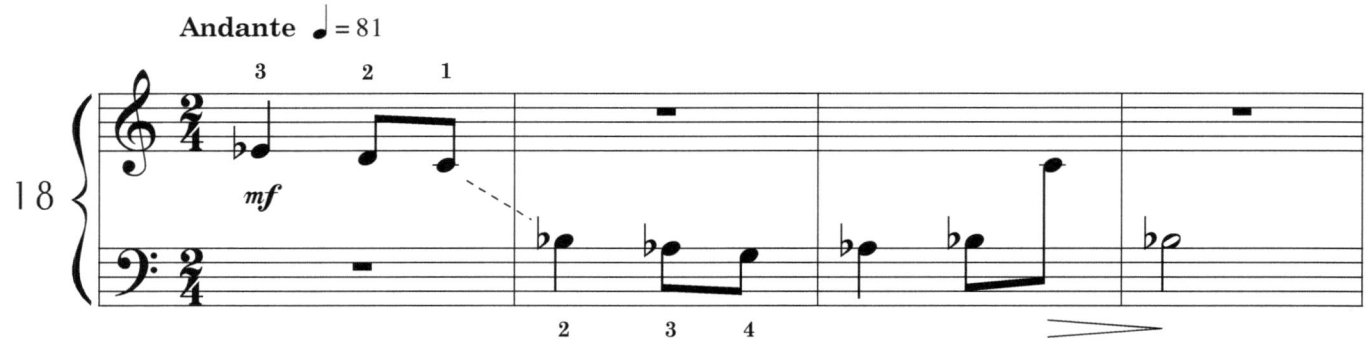

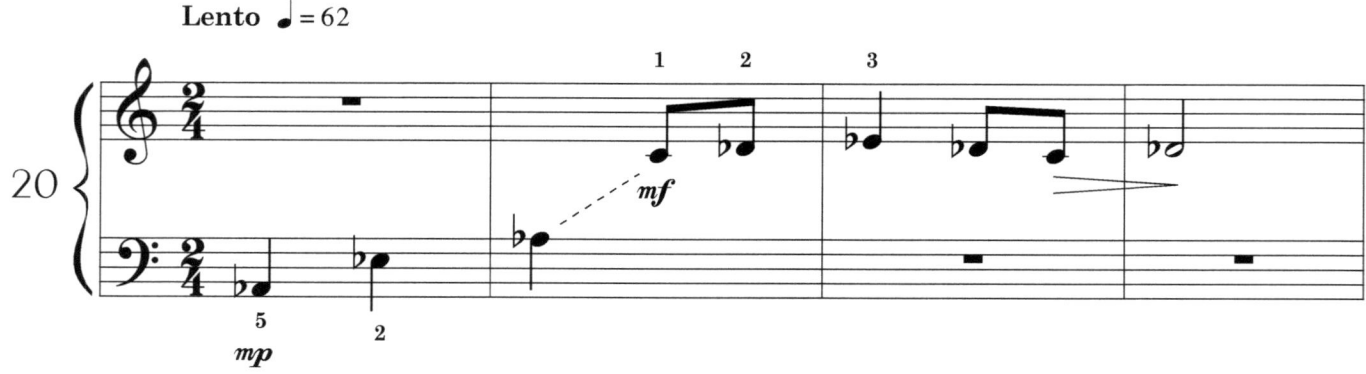

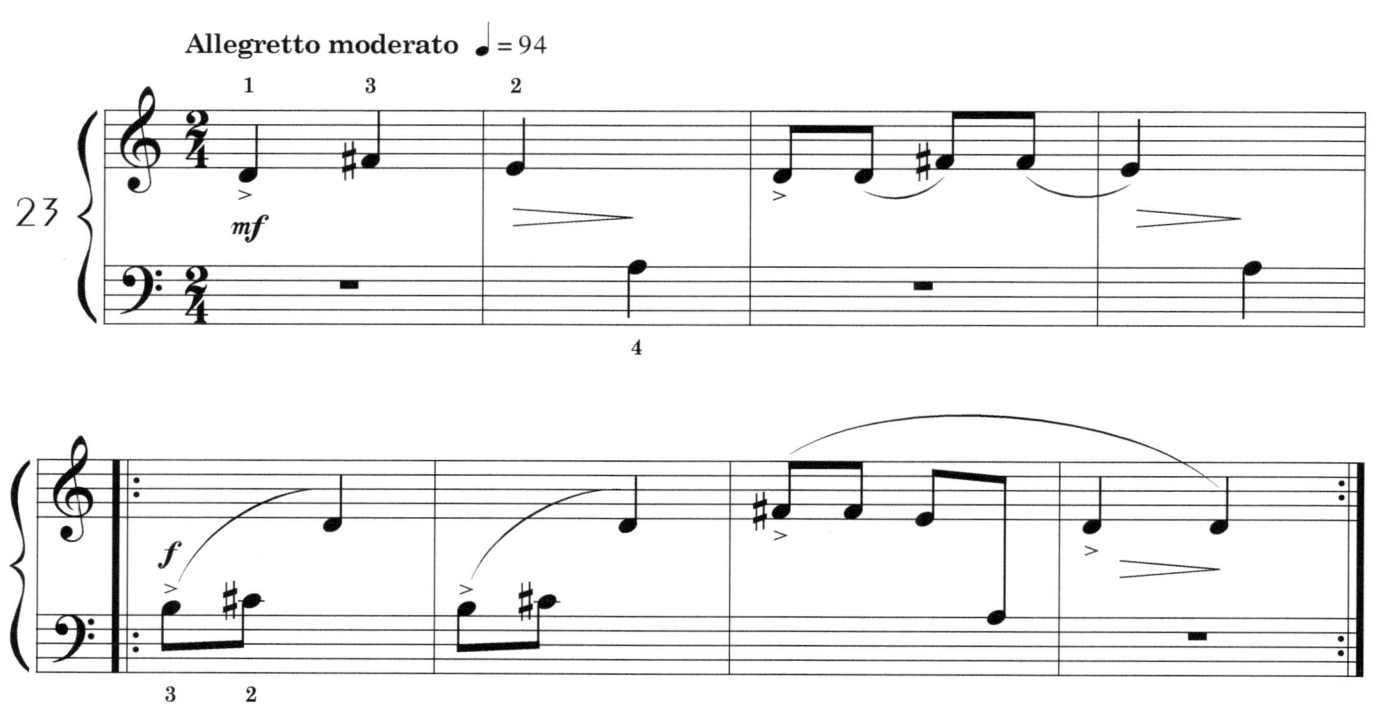
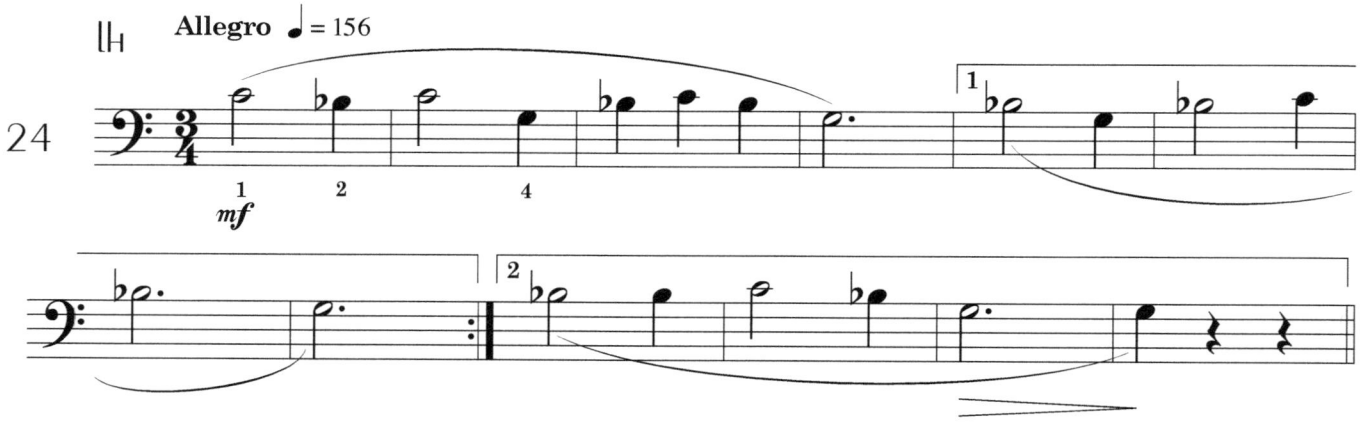
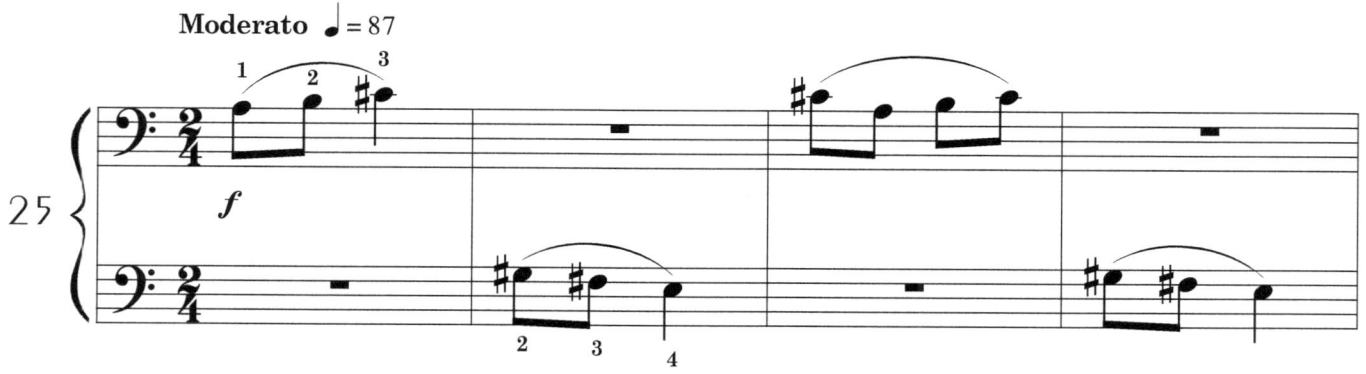

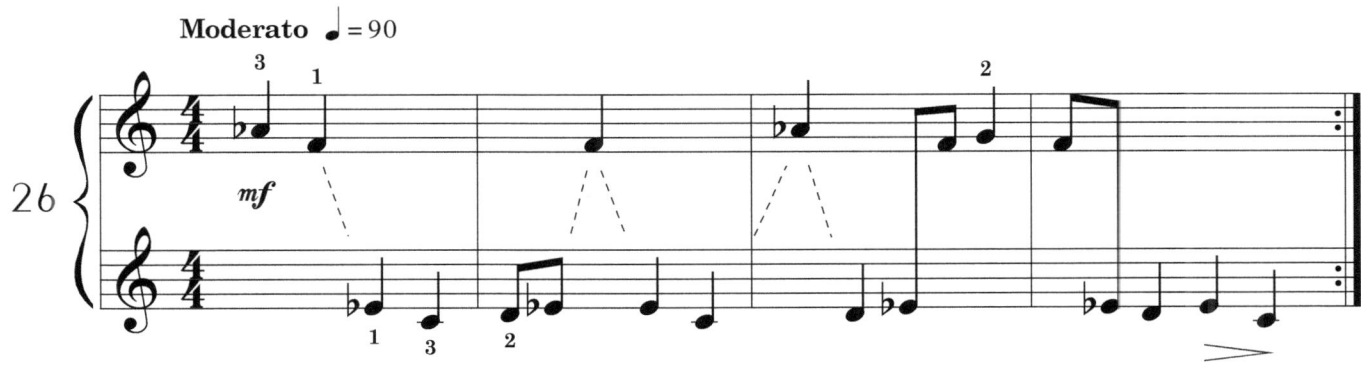

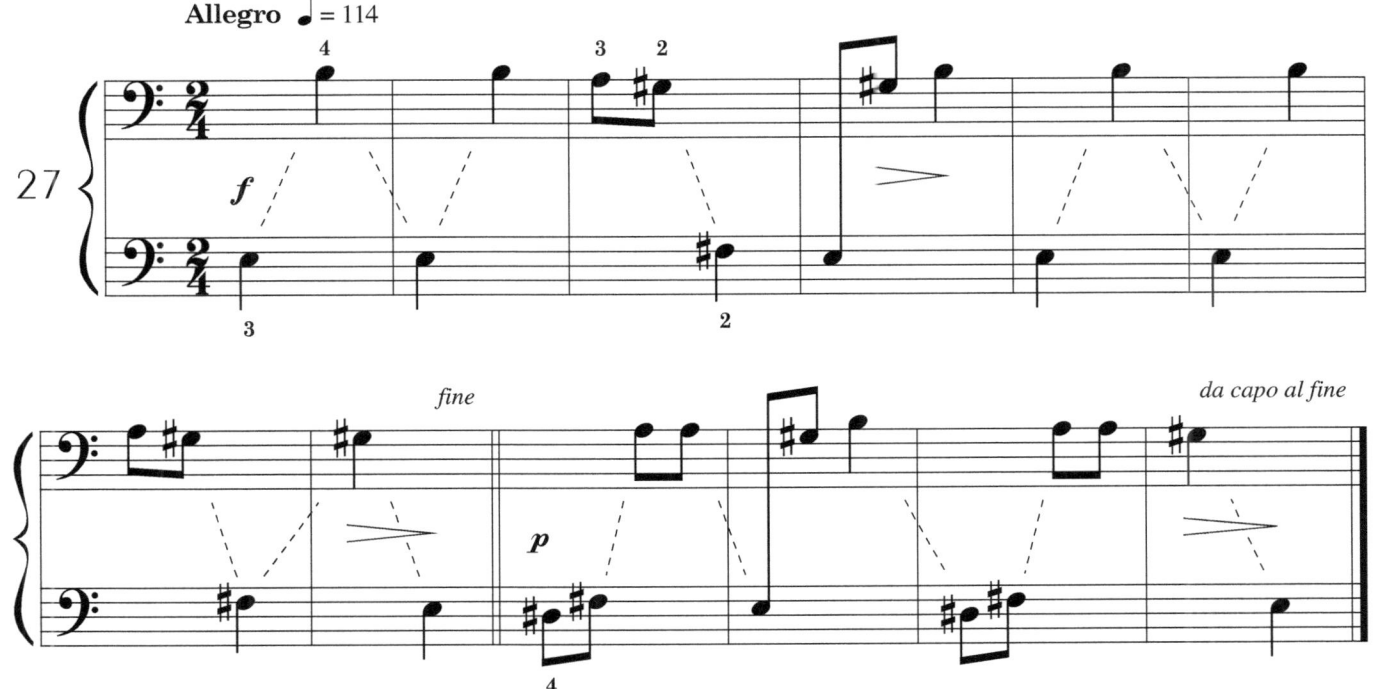

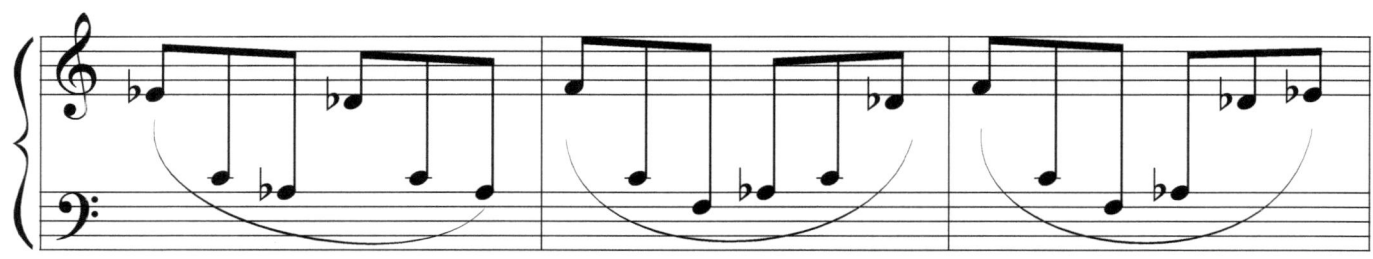
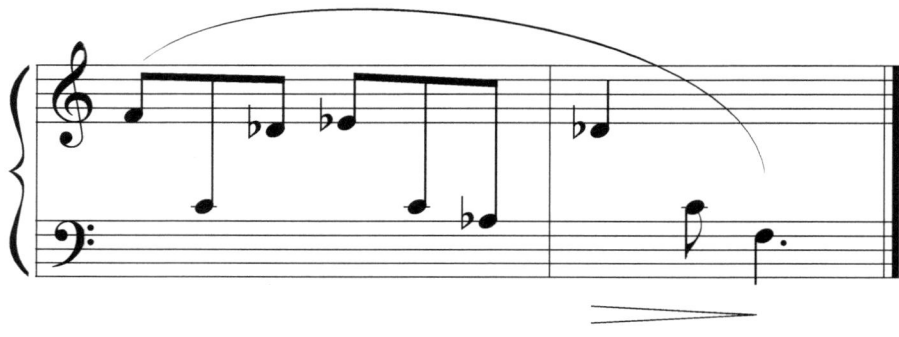

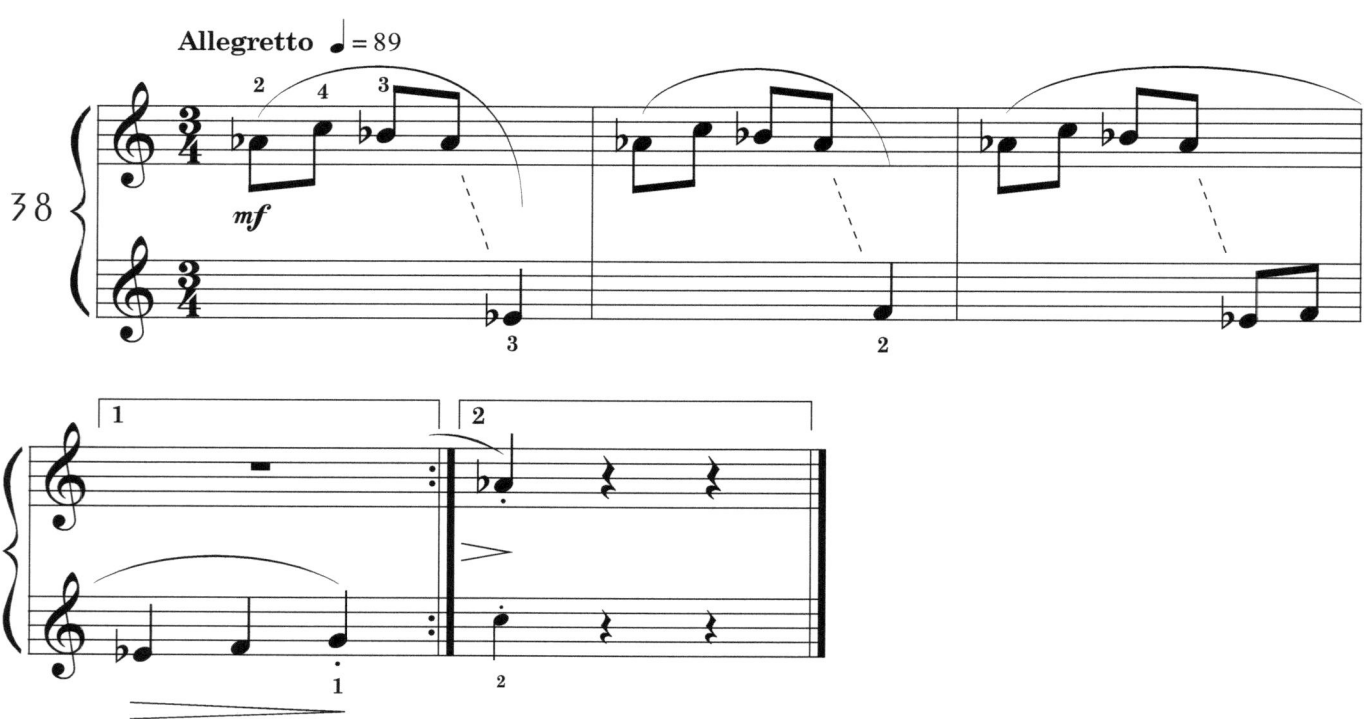

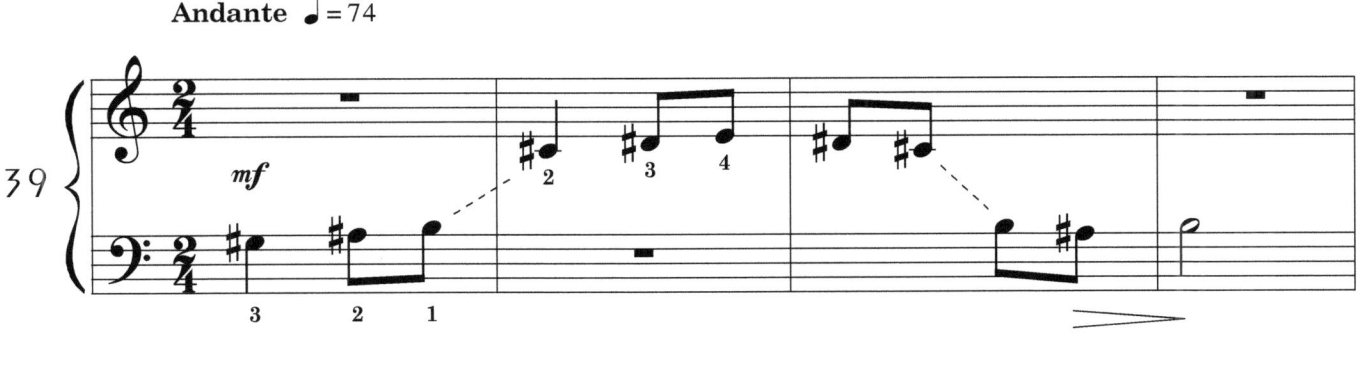

Andante ♩ = 74

41

Moderato ♩. = 63 (♪ = 189)

42

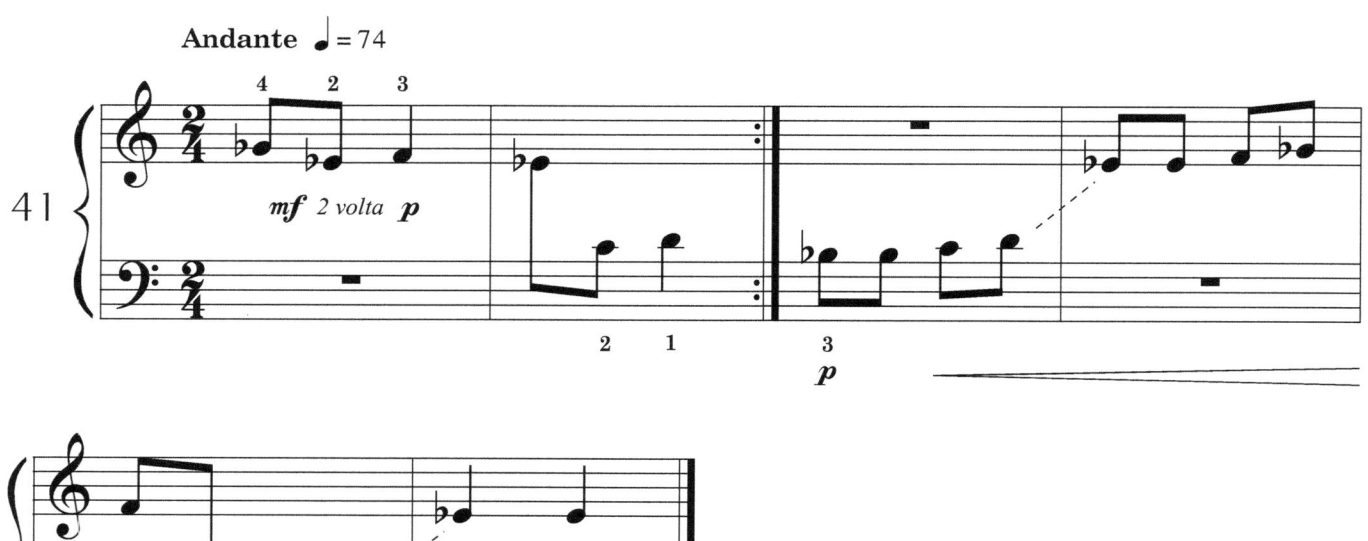

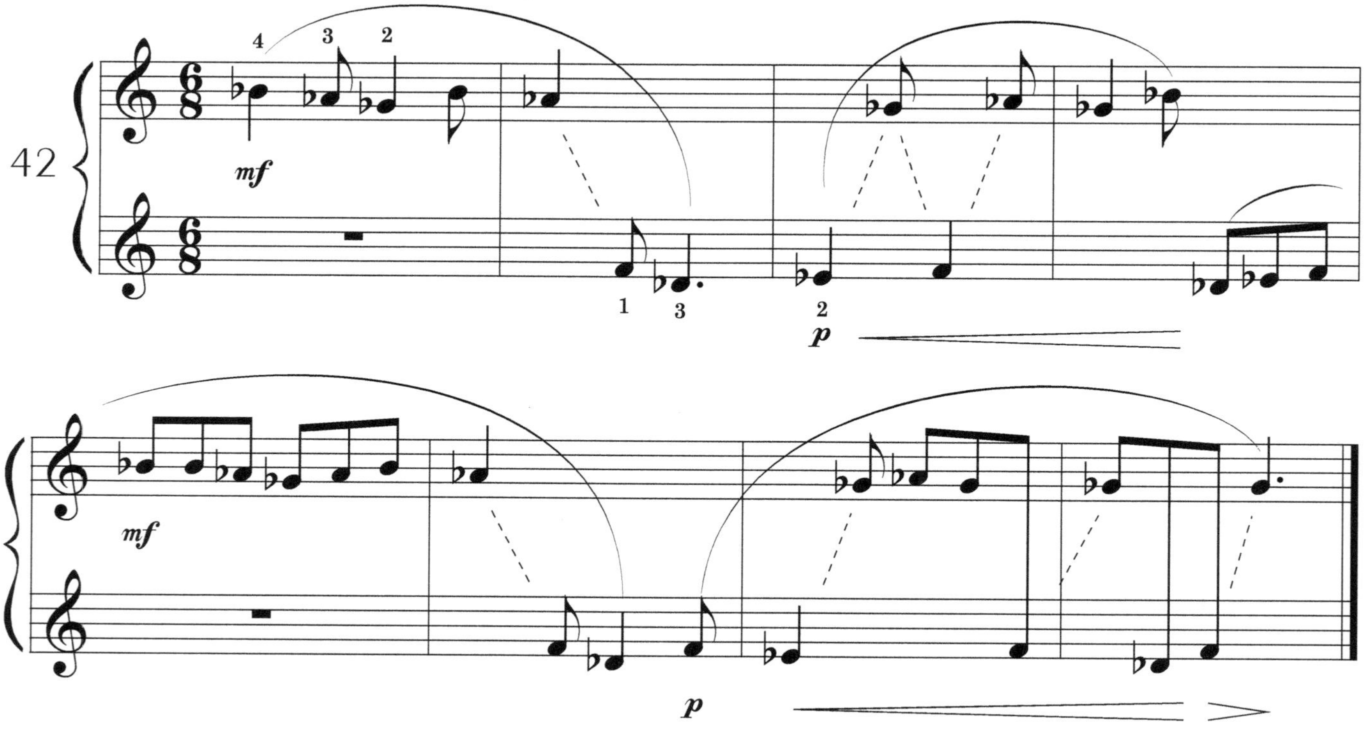

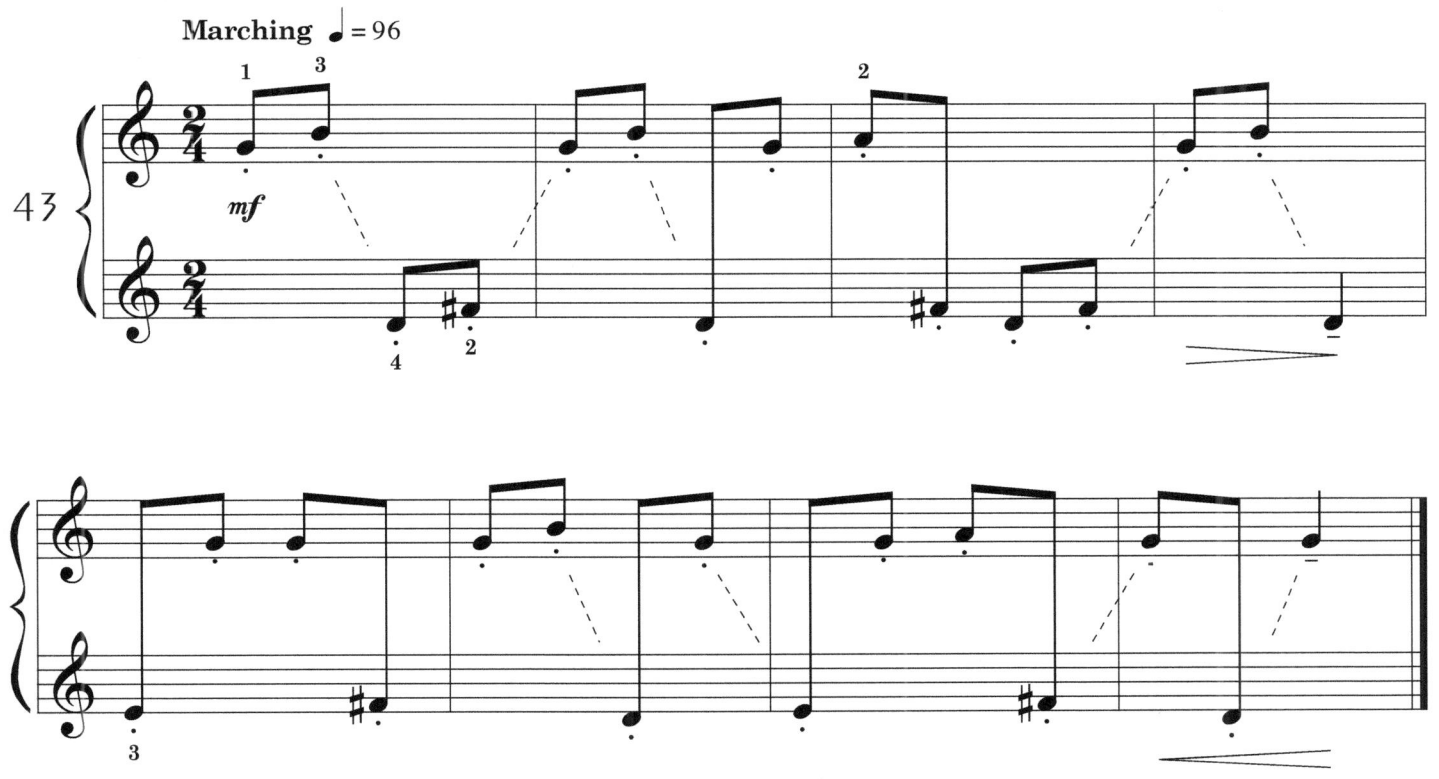

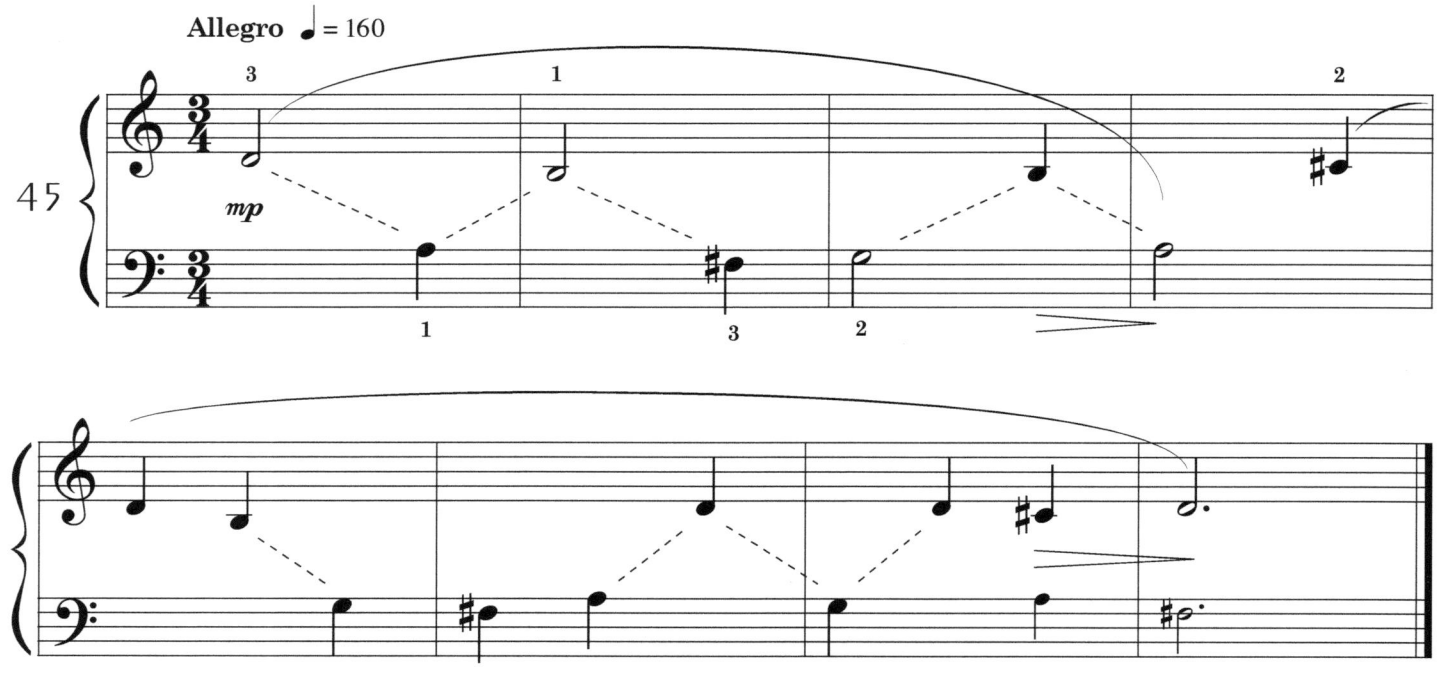
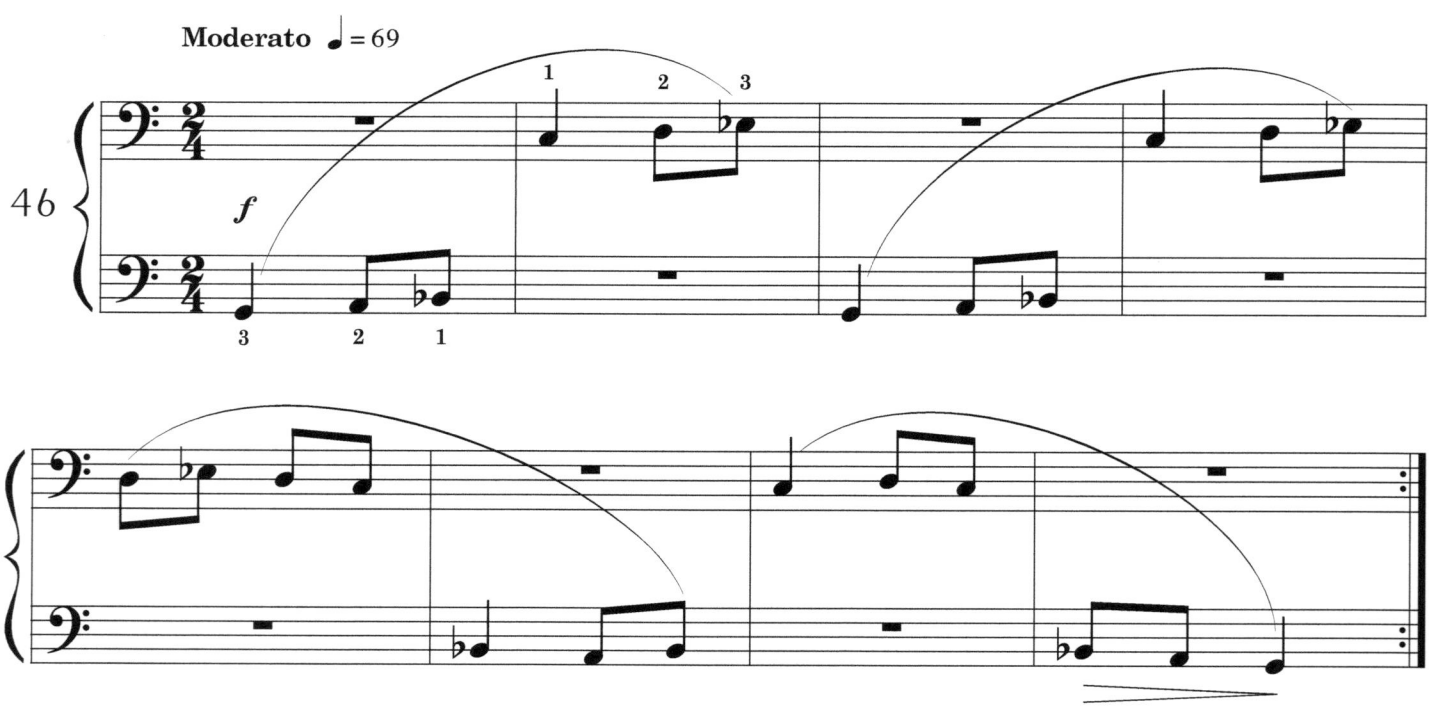

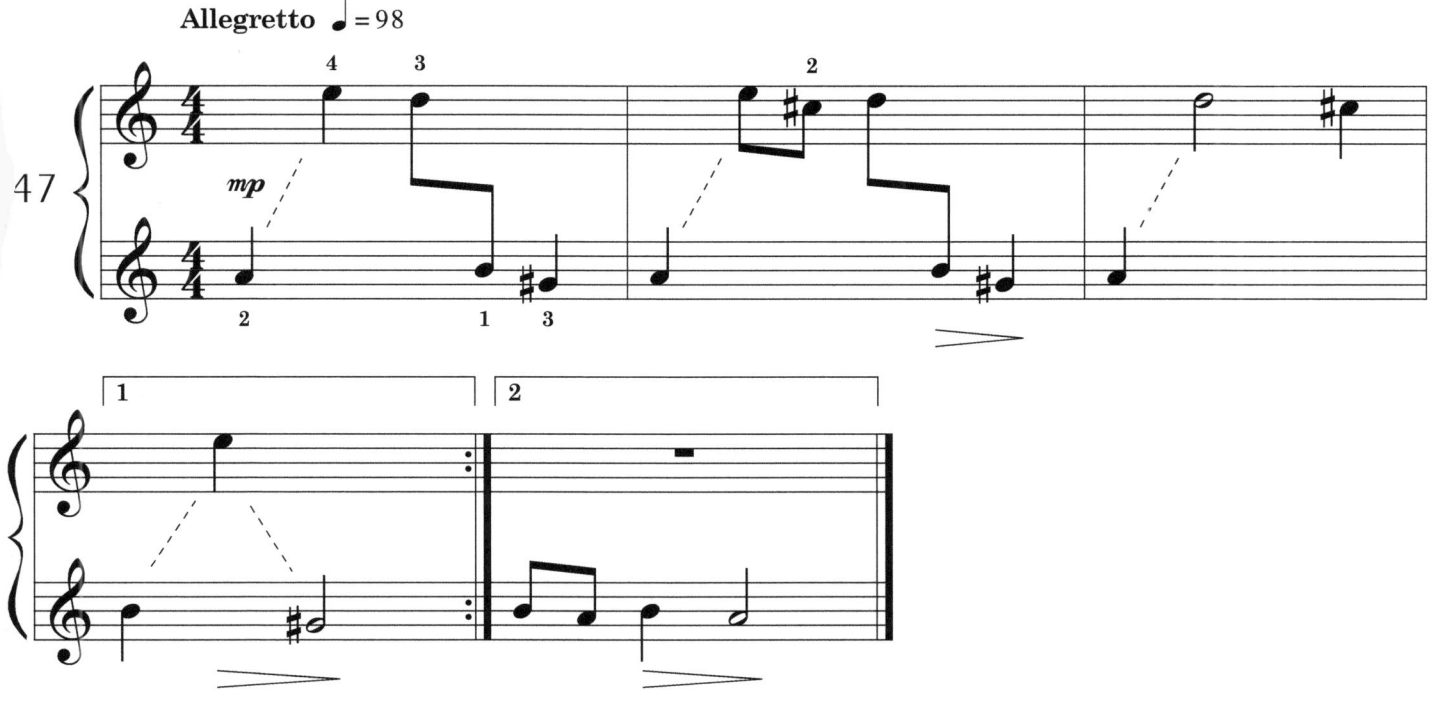
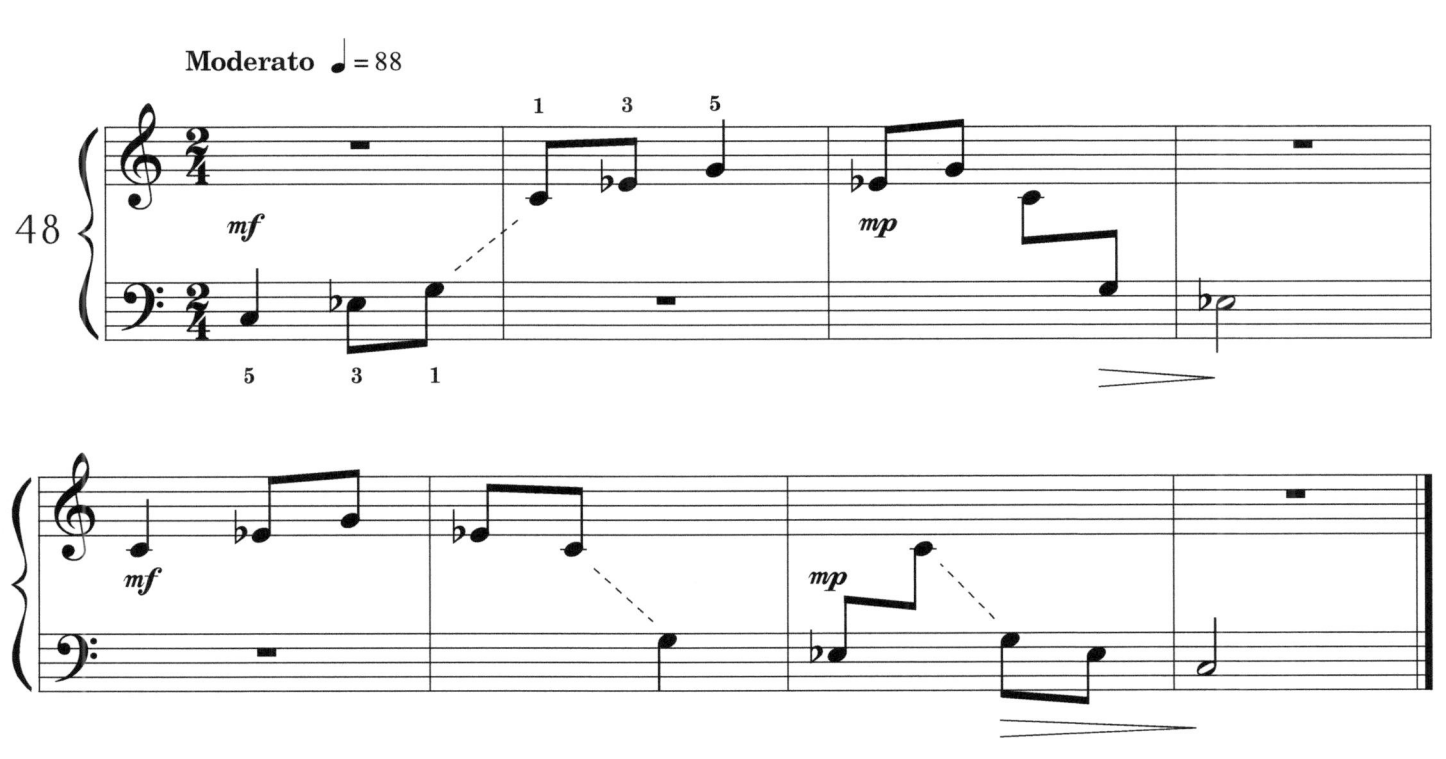

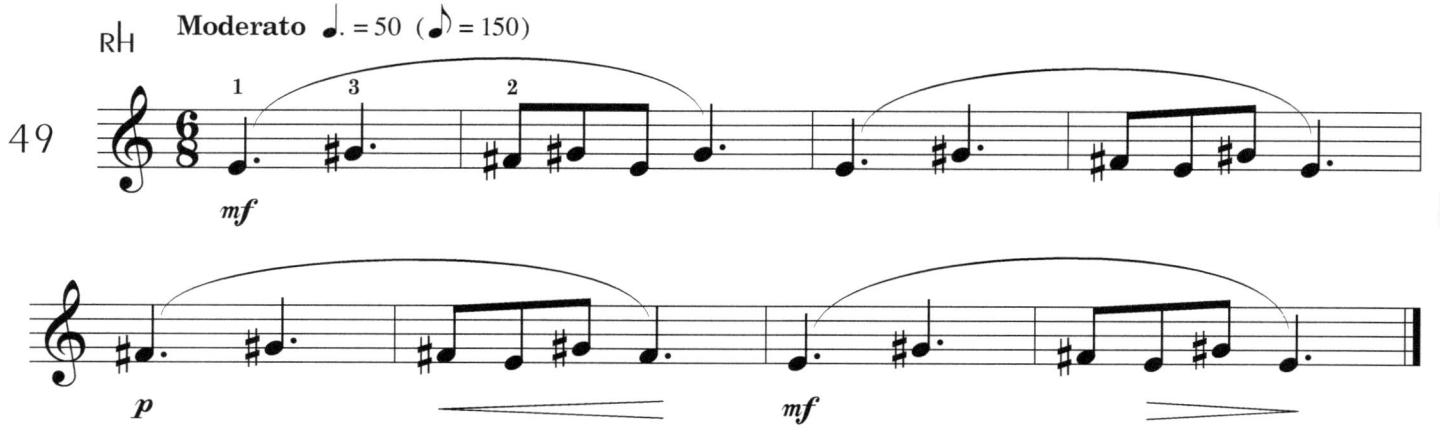